NORTH OF SUMMER

North of Summer

POEMS FROM BAFFIN ISLAND

Alfred Purdy

WITH OIL SKETCHES OF
THE ARCTIC BY

A. Y. Jackson

MCCLELLAND AND STEWART
LIMITED / TORONTO MONTREAL

The Canadian Publishers

McClelland and Stewart Limited
25 Hollinger Road, Toronto 16

PRINTED AND BOUND IN CANADA

TO:
Frank Scott

Contents

Colour plates
by courtesy of
The Beaver
published by
the Hudson's
Bay Company

A Portfolio of Arctic Sketches

BY

A. Y. Jackson

MOUNT ASGARD

BAFFIN ISLAND 1965

BAFFIN ISLAND

FROM CAMP TOWARD HIGHWAY GLACIER

SHORE LINE

FROBISHER BAY 1965

FROBISHER BAY VILLAGE

BAFFIN ISLAND 1965

MOUNT BATTLE

BAFFIN ISLAND 1965

SLOPES OF MOUNT BATTLE

BAFFIN ISLAND 1965

GLACIER LAKE FROZEN

BAFFIN ISLAND 1965

GLACIER LAKE

BAFFIN ISLAND 1965

On the country road these spring days
odd things happen
brown men in mukluks climb
                    the snake fences
with Norris Whitney's sheep
near Ameliasburg
and I'm afraid to mention it
at the village store

The Turning Point

Over northern Canada
daylight ahead and growing
behind only darkness
at 2.30 in the morning
while the d.c.4's engines drone

Suzanne the stewardess
is a French Canadian agnostic
which surprises me a little

Then she says most of her friends
feel the same way about god
and points where the last
darkness lingers
with the moon's silver image
on the silver aircraft

"But I see angels out there sometimes"
"Human angels?" I say
She laughs and talks about going
back to u. of m. to get her m.a.
and I must have said the wrong thing

The full shape of the Arctic moves
under us and flows
into quiet islands and swinging coastlines
blue seas reflecting our tiny aeroplane
the runaway world upside down
and no god of chaos to lift one hand
and make the place behave

Then it's gone completely
we're lost
entombed in wool blankets
and go whispering thru nothingness
without sun or moon
human instruments haywire
But we find another world
a few minutes later
with snow-streaked hills down there
that must be Baffin Island

A club-shaped word
a land most unlike Cathay or Paradise
but a place the birds return to
a name I've remembered since childhood
in the first books I read
a warm kind of wonder in myself
I used to be ashamed of

It's getting cold as hell here
                              I guess
the Arctic is no place for shirtsleeves
The stewardess serves coffee before we land
and looks out the window absentmindedly
"What's your thesis, Suzanne?"

OVER FORT CHIMO — AND LATER AT FROBISHER BAY

The North West Passage

                              is found
needs no more searching
and for lack of anything better to do
waiting the plane's departure north from Frobisher
I lounge on the bed poring over place-names
on maps
                and baby it's cold outside
I amuse myself with the idea of
                              Martin Frobisher
"Admiral of the Ocean-Sea" who was
"hurte . . . in the Buttocke with an Arrowe"
running down the beach near here
to escape the blood-mad Skraelings hoping
to reach Mrs. Frobisher in time for tea
But Frobisher didn't make it either
in 1576
              and it's two hours until dinner
tho I'm not really very hungry just now
Locate Fury and Hecla
              on the orange-coloured paper
north west of where I am on Baffin
and go rocking thru history
in search of dead sailors
suspended from Ariadne's quivering cord
and find them at the precise point
where the meter registers 'alive'
when a living man remembers them
and the Minotaur's bull-roar
trembles in the northern lights
and a red needle flickers
on the playback device

Locate the Terror and Erebus that way
Franklin's ships preserved in ice
with no place-names for them
it'd be much too close to hell

and the big jets might take a wrong turn
skimming over the top of the world
or the ICBM computers make a quarter inch error
and destroy the illusion of paradise by mistake
and Capt. James' letter to the Emperor of Japan
suddenly gets delivered three centuries later
Or take the Ringnes boys
                              Ellef and Amund
heroic Norwegian brewers whose names
cling alcoholically to islands up there
or Boothia after an English gin distiller
Names like Ungava and Thule
                              The Beaufort Sea and Ellesmereland
places to drop cigarette butts in
while the big jets go popping over the horizon
to Moscow and you can snooze 5 minutes
before the stewardess brings dinner
or read the New Yorker with a double whiskey
and make it last a thousand miles
for it's a long time since Luke Foxe's cook
served "beer in small cans" to the sailors
and it didn't last one nautical mile

The North West Passage is found
and poor old Lady Franklin well
she doesn't answer the phone
tho once she traded her tears for ships
to scour the Arctic seas for her husband
but the Terror and Erebus sank long ago
and it's still half an hour before dinner
and there isn't much to do but write letters
and I can't think of anything more to say
about the North West Passage
but I'll think of something
maybe
a break-thru
to strawberries and ice cream for dinner

FROBISHER BAY

21

Arctic River

(The Sylvia Grinnell on Baffin Island)

"From the river I have taken a draught on eating
by its banks American cheese and American bread.
The American flag floats flauntingly over it as the
music of its waters seems to be 'Yankee Doodle.' I
see not why this river should not have an American
name. (He named it) with the flag of my country
in one hand, my other in the limpid stream."

C. F. HALL, 1861

The river is

old as gods as old
when they've forgotten
their last worshipper
Hills mottled with snow
and a criminal look about them
as if they'd killed something
      (water is older than they)
and rapids stampede to the sea
between two icy shores
A dozen kinds of wild flowers
whose names I don't know
where just to be alive is a triumph
they celebrate with yellow
and purple banners underfoot
for a few days in July
      (older than those)
Rock cairns of Eskimo graves
beside the charging river
a fragment of ancient bone and
stone circles marking skin tents
long since hauled down
      (older than they)

Dear Sylvia Grinnell
    (older than you)
whose loves are also mouldering
in Boston or somewhere
    (older than Boston)
for your information the river
is still a 'limpid stream'
    (older than C. F. Hall
    and 'Yankee Doodle'
    and not so noisy)
The hunters who died here
and built rock cairns for their dead
whose being here prevented
alternate things from happening
are brown memories
    (older than memories)
Dear Sylvia River
have you a few moments
to spare of my life
in someone else's mind
when I am less than a memory?

FROBISHER BAY

Girl

Sixteen years old and beautiful
all her white blood boiling red
under the not-brown skin maybe
attending music class in winter a
whaler's hornpipe danced the brown girl white as
she slinks from the crew's quarters back
in the 19th century to flattered husband remembering
a blond sailor later remembering
a dark husband remembering
both of them courting her
                    in 1965

(Twelve years ago I went to Europe
and there was one week I wavered
about going or not going
and never did make a final decision
about going or not tho
        I kept an option always
to jump off the boat at the last minute
        in Le Havre harbour
        and swim
back)

No thought of a non-Christian past
enters her working head pounding
a typewriter waiting
for something to happen listening
        to a truck motor outside
            warm up a few square inches
            of Arctic under the metal or
she sits in the tents of her people sewing
skins and a pricked needle finger shows
her red blood

           neither brown nor white & becoming
becoming without going anywhere while
The People wonder about her
(as the people whose thoughts I read
keep wondering if they're crazy
           as I am and decide
           in the negative)
she becomes
beyond any accidental non-decision or
(at midnight back in the 19th century)
the pawing
           of a blind
                       blood donor
becoming and searching
for what's missing
in both of us

       FROBISHER BAY

Eskimo Graveyard

Walking in glacial litter
frost boils and boulder pavements
of an old river delta
where angry living water
changes its mind every half century
and takes a new direction
to the blue fiord
The Public Works guy I'm with
says you always find good gravel
for concrete near a graveyard
where digging is easy maybe
a footnote on human character
But wrapped in blankets
above ground a dead old woman
(for the last few weeks I'm told)
without a grave marker
And a hundred yards away
the Anglican missionary's grave
with whitewashed cross
that means equally nothing
The river's soft roar
drifts to my ears and changes
tone when the wind changes
ice debris melts at low tide
& the Public Works guy is mildly pleased
with the good gravel we found
for work on the schoolhouse
which won't have to be shipped in
from Montreal
and mosquitoes join happily
in our conversation   Then
he stops to consult
with the construction foreman

I walk on
toward the tents of The People
half a mile away
at one corner of the picture
Mothers with children on their backs
in the clean white parkas
they take such pride in
buying groceries at H.B.C.
boys lounging under the store
in space where timber stilts
hold it above the permafrost
with two of them arm in arm
in the manner of Eskimo friends
After dinner
I walk down among the tents
and happen to think of the old woman
neither wholly among the dead
nor quite gone from the living
and wonder how often
a thought of hers enters the minds
of people she knew before
and what kind of flicker it is
as lights begin to come on
in nightlong twilight
and thoughts of me
occur to the mosquitoes
I keep walking
as if something ought to happen
(I don't know what)
with the sun stretching
a yellow band across the water
from headland to black headland
at high tide in the fiord

sealing in the settlement
as if there was no way out
and indeed there isn't
until the looping Cansos come
dropping thru the mountain doorway
That old woman?
it occurs to me
I might have been thinking
about human bookkeeping
debits and credits that is
or profit and loss
(and laugh at myself)
among the sealed white tents
like glowing swans
hoping
for a most improbable
birth

    PANGNIRTUNG

Trees at the Arctic Circle
(*Salix Cordifolia* – Ground Willow)

They are 18 inches long
or even less
crawling under rocks
grovelling among the lichens
bending and curling to escape
making themselves small
finding new ways to hide
Coward trees
I am angry to see them
like this
not proud of what they are
bowing to weather instead
careful of themselves
worried about the sky
afraid of exposing their limbs
like a Victorian married couple

I call to mind great Douglas firs
I see tall maples waving green
and oaks like gods in autumn gold
the whole horizon jungle dark
and I crouched under that continual night
But these
even the dwarf shrubs of Ontario
mock them
Coward trees

And yet – and yet –
their seed pods glow
like delicate grey earrings
their leaves are veined and intricate
like tiny parkas
They have about three months

to ensure the species does not die
and that's how they spend their time
unbothered by any human opinion
just digging in here and now
sending their roots down down down
And you know it occurs to me
                about 2 feet under
those roots must touch permafrost
ice that remains ice forever
and they use it for their nourishment
use death to remain alive

I see that I've been carried away
in my scorn of the dwarf trees
most foolish in my judgements
To take away the dignity
                of any living thing
even tho it cannot understand
                the scornful words
is to make life itself trivial
and yourself the Pontifex Maximus
                of nullity
I have been stupid in a poem
I will not alter the poem
but let the stupidity remain permanent
as the trees are
in a poem
the dwarf trees of Baffin Island

    PANGNIRTUNG

Postscript to 'Trees at the Arctic Circle'

An inch in diameter at the base
        at most two inches
And some have been alive more than
        a thousand years
when the Zuider Zee was a swamp
before Chaucer and Shakespeare
or Leif the Lucky took his first look
at Vinland
        and sniffed disparagingly
when King John's second look was
somewhat less than enthusiastic while
reading the Magna Carta and knowing
the barons knew and he knew they knew
he couldn't read a single word
    – about that time
a small green leaf appeared on
the tundra and began to manufacture oxygen
unnoticed by anyone
its own witness
a thousand years ago
        one day in August

PANGNIRTUNG

Note: I am informed by an Ottawa biolo-
gist that the Arctic ground willow does
not live 1000 years. But even if it doesn't,
I wanted to include this poem.

Innuit

An old man carving soapstone
at the co-op in Frobisher Bay
and in his faded eyes
it is possible to see them
shadowy figures
past the Dorset and pre-Dorset Cultures
5,000 years ago
if you look closely
But the race-soul has drawn back
drawn back
from settlements and landing fields
from white men
into secret vaults
and catacombs of marrow
bone rooms
that reveal nothing
The Innuit which is to say
           THE PEOPLE
as the Greeks called all foreigners
           barbaroi
something other than themselves
           un-GREEK

so the Innuit
           The People
these unknowable human beings
who have endured 5,000 years
on the edge of the world
a myth from long ago
that reaches into the past
but touches an old man still living
Looking into his eyes
it is possible to see the first hunters
(if you have your own vision)
after the last ice age
moving eastward from Siberia
without dogs or equipment
toward the new country
pausing on the sea-ice
for a moment of rest
then pushing on thru the white smother
– Flying generations
leap and converge on this face
an old man carving soapstone
with the race-soul of The People
THE PEOPLE
moving somewhere
behind his eyes

      PANGNIRTUNG

33

Canso*

Swung by the heels like
Achilles
      dipped in mountains
lowered down from 10,000
feet to nil
and dozens of flintspikes
aimed at me solely with
precambrian intentions oh
not so much flattery eh please

And Toonjiks
        giants from Asia
the stupid people of legends
(actually Dorset and Thule cultures)
who crossed the Bering swing bridge
and built houses of whale ribs
buttocks in cloud country
are still defiant tenants here
with jaeger and gyrfalcon

On the sea bottom under us
        Sedna
mother of all sea mammals
Sedna the One-eyed sits
combing her long hair as
seals swim around her and
icebergs drift by in pack ice
above and below the water a
hinge between the real world
        and the mirror world
where dream-things happen

*Catalina flying boat

Giant's country
the Canso's only a mantoy
dandled by Daedalus
perhaps by Picasso
painted yellow bluebottle i.e.
housefly on the worldtop
lunging over the bright table
cloth and someone high up with
a swatter swings hard and splats and
my heart leapfrogs land ah
                    missed us
                            You –

PANGNIRTUNG

35

Arctic Rhododendrons

They are small purple surprises
in the river's white racket
and after you've seen them
a number of times
in water-places
where their silence seems
related to river-thunder
you think of them as 'noisy flowers'
Years ago
it may have been
that lovers came this way
stopped in the outdoor hotel
to watch the water floorshow
and lying prone together
where the purged green
boils to a white heart
and the shore trembles
like a stone song
with bodies touching
flowers were their conversation
and love the sound of a colour
that lasts two weeks in August
and then dies
except for the three or four
I pressed in a letter
and sent whispering to you

PANGNIRTUNG

36

Metrics

Expecting to arrive at a crowded village
I land on a little rocky island
as a kind of star boarder
in charge of an Eskimo family
and English is not spoken here
At first I think it must be
the place I'm supposed to arrive at and
the facsimile I'd made beforehand didn't match
the real thing
              tho it has
          the same sky and the same sea
as the place in my head
Feeling unsure of myself
I take a fast count of the population
(14 Eskimos   1 white man   some dogs)
as a rational measure to make sure
I'm not a computer with built-in defects
             but a man
with heavy loneliness included
for which there seems no answer
And the brown children peer out
                behind
          small
       snotty
    faces
with secret rules to their games
the hunter breaks out a torn spare tent
his wife sews with a hand machine
among stones and
            into
       it   an
     raise   east
   we   wind
while a blind husky bitch
sniffs at my heels

Now the pictures in my head
of what I'd expected things to be like
start to come true
                    bones everywhere
even inside the tent
that swells in wind like a heart
                    trying to break
loose from flesh and
pieces of animal carcass around
yellow blubber in cold sunlight
a white whale's body in shallow water
on the beach with blood
like smoke
            drifting
                    from the beast face
another island 200 yards away
covered with gaunt starving dogs
climbing the crags like goats apparently
left there for the Arctic summer
to survive or not survive
My lost feelings begin to simmer down
to a take what comes attitude
tho I set up the portable typewriter
on a cardboard box in the tent
for an 'order of things'
            I can stay outside
or join in case of desperation
            and eat some beans
and try to decide if all this is a poem
Brief Arctic twilight
            darkens the stone island
something neither day nor night begins
blue water loses what makes it alive
shadows aren't shadows but proxy things
            that represent things

and I wonder what I represent
(– some hustings of the soul?)
Here I'm alone as I've ever been in my life
a windup gramophone scratching out "You Are
My Sunshine"
                in the next tent
the sea crowded with invisible animals
the horizon full of vague white shapes
of icebergs in whispering lagoons where
Old Squaw ducks are going
                        "ouw-ouw-ouw"
And I think to the other side of that sound
I have to
        because it gathers everything
all the self-deception and phoniness
of my lifetime into an empty place
and the RUNNER IN THE SKIES
I invented
            as symbol of the human spirit
                crashes like a housefly
my only strength is blind will
                        to go on
I think to the other side of that sound
                    "ouw-ouw-ouw"
to the point where I know some damfool ducks
are having a ball out there
                    far out
                        there
where I can't join them
and really it isn't really it isn't
the echo of cosmic emptiness at all
(really it isn't!)
and start typing

    SLAUGHTER BEACH (BROWN'S HARBOUR)

Odysseus in Kikastan

Cruising thru the summer seas
with Slaughter Beach behind us
and the Kikastan Islands ahead
while ice castles go drifting by
in the dark blue water
Jonese steers for the islands
and I soak up reflected sun
with 3 days beard and a hangover
from drinking so much hot tea
and being hospitable if it chokes me
but I hate the damn stuff
Simonie makes some on the Coleman
speeding along in another boat
and Jonesee steers close to get hot tea
for himself and his family
I make a face and refuse mine
while everybody laughs
And for some sad reason I'm happy
lounging lazily on the gunwales
a sort of creative doing nothing
that I make a specialty of
Ice castles drift by in the sunlight
blue and turquoise magic
moulded and shaped by water
One looks like a bowling alley
another like Maple Leaf Gardens
here's a dinosaur's white skeleton
and a landing field for D.C. 4s
and a seagoing hamburger with relish
from Joe's Place at Frobisher
(he'll send your change by dolphin)
a king-size diamond from Tiffany's
no lady will finally wear

And you almost expect a sign
        "Castles for Sale
            Apply at Circe's Island"
They come equipped with obsolete plumbing
and Franklin's ghost behind the stairs
but the most delicate dripping music
mermaids dreaming of being human
an all-girl orchestra's tinkling flutes
on Jonesee's Mediterranean Cruises maybe
What do you say Odysseus
        what do you say?
If sirens sing on the Arctic islands
they come equipped with a pair of flippers
blubber lips for drinking tea
they sport a set of real false whiskers
and a cold cold bed on the floor of the sea
but they're shy of strangers
and their singing teacher
never taught them to hit high C
But the castles
        well that's different
I'll take them over apartments any day
to look at not live in
and have one moved to Côte des Neiges
or a white highriser at King and Bay

But we haul our freight to Kikastan Harbour
north of the treeline south of the pole
the lord mayor dressed in his best new parka
come down to the beach with a big hello
six white whales dance thru a seaweed arbour
and several thousand cordial dogs
plus an Eskimo official greeter

(it must be old home week by god)
and a guy with a CBC loudspeaker
who wants me to say a few words but not
unless I happen to be John Diefenbaker
– which is rather confusing so I explain
that I'm only Odysseus after all
        only Odysseus after all

Well I join the Eskimo Stevedore's Union
we pack our luggage up from the sea
Now I'm hard at work on a new translation
of Homer's Odyssey Arctic-fashion
but Jonesee invites me over for tea

        – and that's what happened

KIKASTAN ISLANDS

When I sat down to Play the Piano

He cometh forth hurriedly from his tent
and looketh for a quiet sequestered vale
he carrieth a roll of violet toilet tissue
and a forerunner goeth ahead to do him honour
yclept a snotty-nosed Eskimo kid
He findeth a quiet glade among great stones
squatteth forthwith and undoeth trousers
"The Irrational Man" by Wm. Barrett in hand
while the other dismisseth mosquitoes
and beginneth the most natural of natural functions
buttocks balanced above the boulders
Then
      dogs[1]
          Dogs[3]
              DOGS[12]
                    all shapes and sizes
all colours and religious persuasion
a plague of dogs rushing in
having been attracted by the philosophic climate
and being wishful to learn about existential dogs
and denial of the self with regard to bitches
But let's call a spade a shovel
therefore there I am I am I think that is
surrounded by a dozen dozen fierce Eskimo dogs
with an inexplicable (to me) appetite
for human excrement
                  Dear Ann Landers
what would you do?
                  Dear Perry Mason
what would you do
                  in a case like this?
Well I'll tell you
NOT A DAMN THING
You just squat there cursing hopelessly
while the kid throws stones

and tries to keep them off and out from under
as a big black husky dashes in
swift as an enemy submarine
white teeth snapping at the anus
I shriek
  and shriek
  (the kid laughs)
  and hold onto my pants
  sans dignity
  sans intellect
  sans Wm. Barrett
  and damn near sans anus
Stand firm little Eskimo kid
it giveth candy if I had any
it giveth a dime in lieu of same
STAND FIRM
Oh avatar of Olympian excellence
noble Eskimo youth do your stuff
Zeus in the Arctic dog pound
Montcalm at Quebec
Horatius at the bridge
Leonidas at Thermopylae
Custer's last stand at Little Big Horn
"KEEP THEM DAMN DOGS OFF
YOU MISERABLE LITTLE BRAT!"

Afterwards
Achilles retreateth without honor
unzippered and sullen
and sulketh in his tent till next time appointed
his anus shrinketh
he escheweth all forms of laxative and physick meanwhile
and prayeth for constipation
addresseth himself to the Eskimo brat miscalled

44

"Lo tho I walk thru the valley of
the shadowy kennels
in the land of permanent ice cream
I will fear no huskies
for thou art with me
and slingeth thy stones forever and ever
thou veritable David
Amen"
P.S. Next time I'm gonna take a gun

KIKASTAN ISLANDS

What can't be Said

The Ladies Auxiliary of Baffin Island
(Kikastan Eskimo Chapter)
comes to visit me every day
They gossip about what's exciting
killer whales out in the harbour
rumored exodus of penguins from Toronto
whether mother love prevents child neurosis
relatives at Ungava having to learn French
and ice exploding bad language in Eskimo
I keep busy serving tea
and don't understand a word
One lady extracts a big floppy breast
from her low-cut evening gown
and shoves it all in her kid's mouth
he bubbles like a milk shake
when we run short of milk for tea
I pantomime using hers
then we sing "You are my Sunshine"
in English and Eskimo at once
with Purdy as guest conductor
They grin at me
I grin back
and we sit there like a bunch of monkeys
about as phony as you can get
I in my small corner of the tent
they in the rest of it
while the dogs howl outside
and harbour ice keeps exploding
Later when it gets colder
one of the ladies
gives me a big piece
of canvas to throw over the tent
and sews it on securely
to keep me warm at night
— What can I say?

KIKASTAN ISLANDS

46

Still Life in a Tent
(Or: Tenting tonight in the old camp ground)

In a cave hollowed out in the rain
near a pile of ghostly groceries
and some books
The wind comes
within two feet of where I'm lying
then stops
waiting
and the canvas bulges

I have a slight fever
temperature of maybe 100
nothing to speak of
but no medicine here
And I have a small fear that changes
shape and size
when I consider what might happen
(canoe trip by sea to Pang
among the waving kelp lines
that anchor somebody's world
maybe the seal towns
or Erewhon and Atlantis
with Jonesee nursing the motor
smiling but irritated
at me for making him
miss the good hunting weather
and myself sick in the bilge)

Waves rumble and rant now
on the still listening beach
pounding motherless bergs
to death on rocks
stranding the big calves
at tidal ebb
A clump of yellow flowers
I noticed this afternoon

must be straining their roots
in the windy twilit night
hoping to hold onto
their few home-inches
(like comic yellow flags
of a 40 acre duchy
between Russia and China)
Oh misery me misery me
I am sick as hell
and so sorry for me
touch my forehead
and swallow carefully
expecting it to hurt
smoke a cigarette
drink some coffee
wish it were brandy
hope for morning
and the big wind howls
Now a berg splits
inside/outside the tent
a dry white noise
wet dogs drift in
and out of hearing
I lie there fevered and
float a single thought out
into a night tinted
with day flowers in my mind
then send a second one
to join the first
and my thoughts travel together
in fevered fantasy
north of summer
with ice become a thousand foot wall
so photo-real it might be
me both here and there
staring up and up
a fevered little man
at that cold altar
where June July and August

are a brief tremor
on god's thermometer
My blood burns and burns
with bells of systole and diastole
tolling over the northland
while I strike cross-capillary
with ham sandwich and thermos
to find the court of the Seal-King
where trader and blind explorer
fumbled along the kelp lines
to reach their graves in a blizzard
or came at last to drown

Here I am again
back from the court of the Seal-King
lying in bed with fever
and I'm so glad to be here
no matter what happens
– riding the wind to Pang
or being bored at Frobisher
(waiting for clearing weather)
I'm so glad to be here
with the chance that comes but once
to any man in his lifetime
to travel deep in himself
to meet himself as a stranger
at the northern end of the world
Now the bullying wind blows faster
the yellow flags rush seaward
the stones cry out like people
as my fever suddenly goes
and the huskies bark like hell
the huskies bark like hell

In a cave hollowed out in the rain
near a pile of ghostly groceries
and some books
morning soon

KIKISTAN ISLANDS

49

Listening

In the scant warmth of Arctic sunlight
lying on pink precambrian granite
a mountaintop became an island
before the first man died
And wind-driven manors of shining ice
pass gleaming by
down Cumberland Sound
on a sea so blue it soaks that word
inside the dark human mind
with quivering molecules of blue
Listening
ear pressed against stone
it isn't quiet but silent
so that the sounds I hear
are not from outside me any longer
but gyrating dancing thoughts
or the small noise my body makes
in its act of living
Listening
where solid granite slopes down
into the water into that silence
at the mountain's foot
my ear following its configurations
into the earth-stone
beneath the sea bottom and on
into another silence
where any impossible sound might be
interpreted as God's voice

Listening
no sound at all
only the dull singing of my own ears
to shield me from the larger silence
listening
reaching under the stone
to the far side of the world
into space and beyond space
no sound
Then a black scream shatters silence
and I am shaken
without knowing why
my body suddenly warm then cold
all in a brief time lag before
brain and eyes inform me
of a white bird flying
above this stone island
who made the sound a moment before
And God had not screamed at the world

    KIKASTAN ISLANDS

Dogsong

Wake at dawn and hear them
in your sleeping bag lying drowsy
mourning voices
running down the scale
all the human equivalents
baritone   bass   contralto
counter tenor   choir boy soprano
coloratura and night club crooner
                          Arctic opera
In pouring rain and seawind
hear them
tearing a seal to rags and ribbons
in bloodied water
hear them
running in packs on stone beaches
follow the leader thru these mountains
from boulder to boulder
stepping delicately
the strong ones
lording it over the others
like robber barons
and whining pups
belly-up to beg for mercy
a motionless ancient encounter
denouement pending

Always hungry
always fighting
among the summer islands
in whipcrack winds of winter
hear them
lifting their heads to the sky
at some invisible signal
Impossible to say it means nothing
not catharsis or outlet
in which they resemble
some unhappy humans
facing the riddle of living
who can't understand it
who'll never understand it
or find an answer
and dogs forget the answer
involved in the singing question
and then forget the question
and think of nothing at all
the shivery sound of nothing at all
being savage sled dogs
who sing at the top of the world

     KIKASTAN ISLANDS

Two Hunters

Winding among the white growlers and turquoise
chessmen in the harbour,
landing among stones with the tide receding,
two hunters:
three days gone for a boatload of seal and char,
$70. worth of skins at H.B.C. –
The dogs and children come to watch them,
but two wives stand a hundred yards away
in separate doorways;
and myself a kind of witness,
but not exactly a reporter,
"kabloona" the white man, memorizing details
outside my tent, with Old Squaw ducks
going "ouw – ouw – ouw" beyond the islands.
On the stone beach
Jonesee strips the hide from a pair of seals,
and throws their lard-white bodies into the water,
for dogs to eat in the bloody shallows.
The two hunters turn with seeming negligence
to the place where their wives are waiting,
standing without expression in separate doorways;
the hunters speak a word or two to their wives
in the soft monosyllables Eskimos use,
as if something flowed under the words
(which weren't really very important),
to Leah and Regally, the waiting women.

I say "Hi" to both the hunters,
and then I'm silent — feeling the continuity
of their lives, almost broken by distance,
sort out essentials of what happened
in each other's absence and join again –
Dogs on the beach are fighting and eating
and roiling the water
                        bloody water,
and one of them yelps away from the battle defeated.
In each doorway the hunters stand with their wives,
as garbage rots slowly, the children play games,
icy chessmen in the harbour rock towards shore,
a muscle of wind leaps from the sky,
then wastes itself against blue water,
simultaneously observed by husbands and wives,
with a white man part of their background,
as the strings draw together again.
After a while they go inside –
On the beach dogs are still fighting
over the bones and shreds of seal meat,
a red pool 10 feet across in the water
is a death-area widening slowly turning blue.
And beyond these islands
other adjustments are being made.

     KIKASTAN ISLANDS

55

Aspects

Sometimes in summer
when it rains
mud and garbage
the shore awash with
blood and stones
slippery from rancid blubber
I think of the whole Arctic
as a used sanitary pad
thrown away
           by a goddess
In winter
        along the beaches
above the treeline
among the castles
of green and silver places
a shivering voiceless dogsong
rising
and five motionless suns
pinned on the black horizon
then a tall god
walks the shoreline
and among The People
          disguised
as a garbage collector

KIKASTAN ISLANDS

56

Eskimo Hunter
(New Style)

In terylene shirt and suspenders
sun glasses and binoculars
Peterborough boat and Evinrude motor
Remington rifle with telescope sight
making hot tea on a Coleman stove
scanning the sea and shore for anything
that moves and lives and breathes
and so betrays itself
one way or another
All we need in the line of further equipment
is a sexy blonde in a bikini
trailing her hand thru the sunlit water
maybe a gaggle of Hollywood photographers
snapping pictures and smoking
nationally advertised brands
Like bwana in Africa
pukka sahib in Bengal
staked out on a tree platform
a tethered goat underneath wailing
Papa Hemingway's bearded ghost on safari
or fishing for giant turtles in Pango Pango
      Maybe it is phony
(and all we're after is seal)
but over the skyline
where the bergs heave and glimmer
under the glacier's foot
or down the fiord's blue water
      even under the boat itself
anywhere the unhappened instant is
real blood
      death for someone or some thing
      and it's reassuringly old fashioned

KIKASTAN ISLANDS

Dead Seal

He looks like a fat little old man
an 'Old Bill'   sort of face
both wise and senile   at the same time
with an anxious to please expression
                in fact a clown
which is belied on account of the dark slow worm
of blood crawling down his forehead
that precludes laughter
or being anything   but a dead animal
tho perhaps part of a fur coat

Often I want to pet something
that looks like this
(and been warned the Eskimo dogs are dangerous)
which appeals to me on common ground i.e.
they unsure of what being an animal consists of
I equally unsure of what a human being is supposed to be
(despite the legal and moral injunctions that say
                "Thou Shalt Not"
nobody says or is likely to say with real conviction
                "Thou Shalt – go ahead and Shalt"
                or 'shall' as the case may be)
On the other hand it would be ridiculous
to pat the head of a dead seal
touch the wet blood that streams back from the boat
a feather of smoky brown in the water widening
into a crude trailing isosceles triangle
with mathematically impossible fish
re-tracing the seal's ghost past not
knowing they're involved in anything

And here he is now
                              casually taking a nap
with flippers like futile baby hands
and clown look   of just pretending
                              I shan't wake him
for it would be disgusting to touch the blood
and it's unnecessary to prove anything
even to myself
                              Then change my mind
                              "I (damn well) Shalt"
– reach out as if the head were electric
with a death-taboo invisibly attached
dark and dank-cold with the hair on it
sticky where the bullet touched
                                          less gently
smooth elsewhere like an intimate part
                              of the human body
that must be touched with delight in living
not curiosity and defiance of breaking rules
– But I am no hunter
                              of any kind
go back to the tent
                              to sit for a few minutes
inside the white canvas blindfold and wonder
what got into me?

KIKASTAN ISLANDS

South

Sitting in the boat with an Eskimo hunter
high on the Arctic sea
    and suddenly feel myself
    at the sheer top of the world
    continents reeling away
                  far beneath me
Old Europe
    older Asia
        young America
           timeless Africa
              new-born Australia
             et cetera
for the world IS et cetera
in relation to the Arctic with
tidal coastlines gathered
together down there from
        my illusion
          of u$_\mathrm{P}$n$^\mathrm{e}$s$^\mathrm{s}$
which has no east or west or anything
to do with roads lakes oceans deserts
et cetera
      the world is simply
           South

And the world shrinks away from me
gathers itself as a ghostly premise
      in my own head
tragedy comedy boredom love
      impersonal abstractions here
      objectively mixed together
      without correlatives

But the match I strike and flick at the water
conceivably could circle the hemispheres
the shout I shout could travel thru mountains
tremble down moving glaciers there finding
still hissing skeletons of ancient reptiles
frozen mammoths under the mile-deep ice cap
half a step short of where they were going
and scribble a singing decibel on eternity
search out an Ultimate Listener
                    the Seal-King
lording it over the pack ice

Myself
      elated by the grandiose
      standing up in the boat
      reciting a poem to Jonesee
      the Eskimo hunter
      tho he doesn't understand it
      waving my arms and declaiming
      intonations nuances and everything
      ad lib a line when I stumble
            recover magnificently
      Laurence Olivier feeling his oatmeal
      Alec Guiness unsober at Stratford
      Henry Irving rambunctious on Broadway
            and ad nauseam
I don't know how my Eskimo hunter feels
whether he's embarassed a little
or simply wants to applaud a fine performance
but the icebergs drift away South
to find an interesting coffee house
          and Jonesee giggles
              Jonesee — giggles

Reaction sets in and
brooding by the gunwales
I think of Schopenhauer's "The World
as Will and Idea" and
          whatever the hell the rest of it is
take no account of time and external events
                    until
Jonesee's sudden gun goes "Boom-Boom" and

          ALLAKAZAM
                    a seal

the small whiskered comic dead face
          the Eskimo hunter and his weapons
          and a middle aged white man
          in an open boat together
and seal blood drifting down
the ocean currents to touch
shores of continents
an idea for animals
The seal being not quite dead is
properly whacked with a paddle and
the whiskered innocent surprised face
          supplies a choice of morals

A choice of morals?
Hey Jonesee
          reach over the package
          of whale sandwiches
          pass me the sackbutt
          of fermented blubber juice
and drink a toast to the world
drink to all our illusions
the power of necessity and the competitive idea
that made you a great hunter
in the era of welfare cheques and family allowance

a toast to the pessimists
like Housman and Schopenhauer
and the optimists
such as Leibniz and Robert Browning
drink to the twenty names for snow
and the million names of god
Baalbek Enlil Bel-Marduk Vishnu Shiva drink
to Ishtar Osiris Horus Quetzacoatl and
            Lyndon B. Johnson
to Sedna the One-eyed combing her long hair
on the sea bottom under the icebergs drink
            to them and to Jonesee
            the archetypal hunter
            Hey Jonesee
are you listening?

Somewhat later
            stand up in the boat observing
            the practical necessity of water
            finding its own level
            easing the left kidney
                    especially
reverse blessing on the world
from a sacriligeous well-wisher
impure joy and powerful impulse
love and hate together
a libation from the Arctic
blood of a most experienced lambkin
stand up in the boat rocking gently
in all directions South
             and say
           "Look out down there!"

KIKASTAN ISLANDS

63

Washday

An oil drum full
of greasy water simmering
all morning with
a blubber fire
underneath
Two women dip
water into plastic tubs
then scrub by hand
with store detergent
I stand and watch
then join the scrubbing
myself
for no reason or any
I can think of
and work at the clothes
seriously as hell
And Leah laughs
her smooth broad face
convulsed with it
a small saliva bubble
blown from her lips
and even Regally
so much darker and quiet
concedes a smile
I think then
even without knowing
the language at all
it's possible to speak

to them
       dark hair falling
in Leah's eyes as
she laughs and brushes
it back giving me
washday instruction
the baby asleep
on her back
Regally impatient
at this foolery
her standing darkness
looms over me like speech
disapprovingly
They chatter about it
in Eskimo
and I try to figure out
what they're saying
remembering I read somewhere
how they add syllable to
syllable so
that a sentence
is just one long word
that keeps being added to
or something like that
Leah still smiling
over the crazy visitor
who wants to wash her clothes
brown eyes and

deep dimples in cheeks
she keeps talking
Suddenly I
feel I'm picked up
with surprised vertigo
and held
between those lips
as she adds my name
to the weightless sounds
breathed out
some of the 'me' I am
removed
the walled self
defenses down
altered
I'm given to the air
then back to myself
like a gift from her
On impulse
I say
        "Leah"
and stop then
but she looks at me
queerly
And wind promenades
among the tents
wrestles with canvas
and the dogs
shit around us

KIKASTAN ISLANDS

Kikastan Communications

Sitting on my air mattress
in the tent
hunting for common ground
some word gesture or runes
in the tea leaves
we all understand
I improvise brilliantly
and the two Eskimo women laugh
amused by odd sounds in my throat
strange vocal doodles
as my adam's apple bobs
up and down like water coming
deep down in an old wooden pump
that sounds something like "guáy-au-góu"
a memory summoned from childhood
when for other kids
it was everyday magic
that made things happen
and then unhappen
No women far south would be so amused
they'd think I was a child
and I am a child
hunting for other children
in a happy grunting language
subversive to commonsense
I'm betrayed by an audience
of Leah's warm brown eyes
whose syntax is the sun and moon
and Regally's quite obvious
displeasure at her own pleasure
and I remain a puzzle to myself
a grey-haired child
– Outside the other hunters are coming
announced by the wise dogs

KIKASTAN ISLANDS

Tent Rings

Stones in a circle
on an island in the Kikastan group
placed there long ago
to hold down the skirts
of caribou skin tents
All over the Arctic
these tent rings
going back thousands of years
in the land where nothing changes
The Dorset People of Baffin
nomads down the centuries
in hustling seawind
left them and journied on
Thule people of Greenland
and the wild Skraelings
of Norse legend
wanderers among the islands
in the Beaufort Sea
left such rings of stone
The radioactive detective
Carbon 14 provides no calendar
tho it dates horn scrapers
ivory spear heads
and bones of men
Here's another one
weathered granite boulders
from the Precambrian
before there was life at all
arranged here fifty years ago
or several thousand
In some sense I think of them
as still here in the circle
the small brown men
they lived so strongly

with such a gift of laughter
the morning sun touches
and glances off
their sparkling ghosts
To enter these tent rings
is mingling with the past
being in two places
having visions
hearing voices
sounding in your head
almost like madness
summoned by wizard angakoks
a thousand year old spell
relayed and handed down
a legacy
from dead to the living
Turning away from here
now in the future I suppose
the stones will be rectangular
even octagonal maybe
having the shape of canvas tents
that came from white traders
and some visitor
in the far future
(probably non-human)
will notice them
and not know whether
they belonged to the Innuit
the "men pre-eminently"
or white men
who were also visitors
and thought to be human

    KIKASTAN ISLANDS

69

Track Meet at Pangnirtung

The young Eskimo mothers
line up for a foot race leaving
babies with the old women
When the Anglican minister says
                              GO
they gallop like rainbows
a dozen of them
in white parkas with red and blue trim
laughing and panting to   the finish line to
reclaim their babies
A white construction worker gives
one old woman a package of cigarettes as
payment for taking her picture so
she smiles   a smile from her ancient youth
he takes away with him
                    into the leapfrog future
The different age groups of children
line up for sack races
            and piggyback races
                    boy and girl races
and the husbands lounge off to one side
trying to act as if they don't enjoy it
all of them

sea hunters from the hungry islands
      now weaponless
No one seems to mind losing here
for losing is a kind of pleasure when
a wounded seal doesn't swim away
      under the ice
        and laughter is
a red filling between the hours
laughter is
ignorant wisdom of the young
as the old men in their bones
know
      having laughed many times
      with serious faces still
      in the running

PANGNIRTUNG

What do the Birds Think?

Are they exiles here from the rest of the world?
Déjà vu past egg and atom
from the yellow Sahara-ocean
or farmlands in Ontario
a witness   hanging   daubed
in the rural blue
while a plowman half a mile down
in the dark field with a snoring tractor
moves in circular sleep?
Or exiles from the apple country
where Macs and Spies plop soft
on wet ground in slow autumn days
with the rotten tangy odour
of cider rising on moonwept nights?
Have they lists and a summary
of things elsewhere and
remember the crimson racket
encountering tropic strangers
or nests of an old absence
lined with a downy part of themselves
far south?
And being south do they think sometimes
of the rain and mists of Baffin
and long migrations wingtip to wingtip
a mile high
and mate to mate in the lift and tremble
of windy muscles pushing them
pushing them where?
And do they ever
an arrow leader pointing the way
touch wearily down on ships passing?
– "Rest here a while and go on!"
(Forgotten in the hurry
of their streaming generations

another captain
called Noah
& Bjarni Herjolffson
in horned helmet
and the sweeps' silver lifting
to a luring Hyperborean ocean
or whaling ships' myopic stumbling
from dull wave to dull wave and the
paint of the bright-over-the-horizon-gazing
woman flaked with salt)
How are we kept here
by what bonds
are we always exiles
a chirping roar in the silence
of foxes and watery romp of walrus
in the long sea lands
or perched on rubbery muskeg
like blue teacups
or lost brown mittens
by what agency of restlessness
in the driftwood heart?
Until on a day the eggs hatch
and the young are trained to endurance
ice rattles the shroud of summer
the flight plans sent
the log book sand is scribbled on
"Goodbye — we are going — Hurry"
and mounting a shaft of sunlight or
the mizzen mast of the sky
they climb and go
And that is the way it is?
Except perhaps I wonder
do they ever
remember down there in the southland
Cumberland Sound
and the white places
of Baffin
that I will remember soon?

  PANGNIRTUNG

73

H. B. C. Post

Here Eskimos come with sealskins,
the bread and butter of the Arctic,
a rare polar bear, some fox maybe –
They bring in a bundle of furs
and throw it on the floor,
then look at the post manager:
$7. is the price for a good ring seal,
$14. for the glossy patterned harp seal:
but many have bullet holes
or other imperfections –
The h.b.c. man inspects the furs,
decides on a fair price and notes it down,
hands the slip of paper
with an offered amount to the hunter.
Then a slight pause,
as one optimistic estimate meets
the concrete fact of the money they're worth.
No bargaining at all.   But the manager talks
to the hunter in his own language,
explains the reasons behind his price,
picks out a fault here and another there,
and the transaction ends with acceptance,
and another hunter is waiting.
But in the Eskimo's mind I have seen
clothes for the whole family,
new rifles with telescopic sights,
100 pound sacks of flour and groceries,
shining marine engines, clean white tents,
stacked up dream-high in his mind
                    come tumbling down –

PANGNIRTUNG

74

The Sculptors

Going thru cases and cases
of Eskimo sculpture
returned from Frobisher
because they said it wasn't
good enough for sale to
T. Eaton Co. Ltd.
Getting itchy excelsior packing
inside my shirt and searching
for one good carving
one piece that says "I AM"
to keep a southern promise
One 6-inch walrus (tusk broken)
cribbage board (ivory inlay gone)
dog that has to be labeled dog
polar bear (badly crippled)
what might be a seal (minus flipper)
and I'm getting tired of this
looking for something
not knowing what it is
But I guess they got tired too
looking for rabbit or bear
with blisters from carving tools
dime-sized and inflating
into quarters on their fingers
waiting
for walrus or white whale
under the ice floes to
flop alive on their lap
with twitching animal faces
unready to taste the
shoe blacking carvers use
for stone polish
I'm a little ashamed of myself
for being impatient with them
but there must be something
there must be something

one piece that glows
one slap-happy idiot seal
alien to the whole seal-nation
one anthropomorphic walrus
singing Hallelujah I'm a Bum
in a whiskey baritone
But they're all flawed
broken
      bent
          misshapen
failed animals
with vital parts missing
And I have a sudden vision
of the carvers themselves
in this broken sculpture
as if the time & the place & me
had clicked into brief alignment
and a switch pulled
so that I can see and feel
what it was like to be them
the tb out-patients
failed hunters
who make a noise at the wrong time
or think of something else
at the trigger moment
and shine their eyes
into a continual tomorrow
the losers and failures
who never do anything right
and never will
the unlucky ones
always on the verge
of a tremendous discovery
who finally fail to deceive
even themselves as time begins
to hover around them
the old the old the old
who carve in their own image
of maimed animals
And I'd like to buy every damn case

PANGNIRTUNG

At the Movies

The setting is really unreal
about 150 Eskimos and whites
jammed into a Nissen hut to
watch Gary Cooper and Burt Lancaster
in a technicolour western shootemup
Eskimos don't understand the dialogue
at all but they like the action
and when noble Gary is in danger
or sinister Lancaster acts menacing
a tide of emotion sweeps the hot little hut
and kids crawling on the floor are quiet
sensing what their parents feel
that something tremendously important is happening
When the Anglican minister changes reels
(his blond head glinting as he administers
spiritual unction to his flock)
cigarettes are lit and everyone talks and
a kid crawls under my legs grinning bashfully
Jim Kilabuk says something I can't quite hear
a baby cries in the pouch on his mother's back
and is joggled gently
It's hot and stuffy as hell in the theatre
doors have to be opened
the odour of white and Eskimo
making a point for air conditioning
Lights go out and Gary Cooper rides again
the forces of evil are finally defeated
only the virtuous bullet kills
violence neutralizes violence
like a mustard plaster
(tho I kinda like the bad guy)
the way it always does in American movies
with an obvious moral a clear-cut denouement
Outside the fiord looks like poured blue milk
mountains like bookmarks under a cold sky

77

islands are moonscapes
where this story happens
It's 11 p.m.
some of the hunters visit their boats
where dead caribou drain into bilgewater
and the rest of the moviegoers go
home to tents on the beach or prefab houses
and dogs howl to make everything regional
But the point I'd hoped to separate
from all these factual things stubbornly
resists me and I walk home slowly feeling stupid
rejecting the obvious
threading my way between stones in the mud
with the beginnings of a headache

    PANGNIRTUNG

The Country of the Young

A. Y. Jackson for instance
83 years old
halfway up a mountain
standing in a patch of snow
to paint a picture that says
"Look here
You've never seen this country
it's not the way you thought it was
Look again"
And boozy traders
lost in a dream of money
crews of homesick seamen
moored to a China-vision
hunting the North West Passage
they didn't see it either
The colours I mean
for they're not bright Gauguin
or blazing Vincent
not even Breughel's "Hunters in the Snow"
where you can get lost
and found in 5 minutes
— but the original colour-matrix
that after a giant's heartbeat
lighted the maple forests
in the country south
You have to stoop a little
bend over and then look up
– dull orange on a cliff face
that says iron deposits
olive leaves of the ground willow
with grey silver catkins
minute wild flower beacons
sea blue as the world's eye –

And you can't be looking for something else
money or a night's lodging on earth
a stepping stone to death maybe
or you'll never find the place
hear an old man's voice
in the country of the young
that says
      "Look here –"

PANGNIRTUNG

Postscript

I spent most of the summer in 1965 on Baffin Island, flying from Montreal to Frobisher Bay (Baffin) by Nordair D.C. 4. From Frobisher I flew to Pangnirtung near the Arctic Circle, taking along a full set of Arctic clothing and a forty-ounce bottle of liquor in case of snakebite. I had it stuffed up my sleeve along with an arm when we circled the mountains to land at Pang, not being sure that prohibition wasn't in effect thru the north. Times might have changed since Robert Service.

In Pang I stayed at the hostel for Eskimo schoolchildren, wandered all over the settlement of two hundred Eskimos and whites by day, and sat up half the night writing. I enjoyed myself tremendously. Everything about the north was new and strange to me, despite having read about it in books beforehand. None of the travel books about the north gave me a specific sense of place, being more concerned with fact and not impression, size and not colour, information and not feeling.

Around the settlement at Pang, mountains rose sheer from the blue fiord. I climbed a small one, said to be less than three thousand feet high. I thought it would take only an hour or so, but the damn thing stretched out like an accordion the higher I got, including wide tundra meadows, fields paved with boulders, even a small ice-covered lake about halfway up.

After a few weeks in Pang I began to think I hadn't really arrived at the last frontier, and wanted to find some place where Eskimos lived the way they did before there were white men in the north. Wayne Morrison, the Canadian Government's regional administrator, arranged that I should go along with an Eskimo family to live with them on the Kikastan Islands in Cumberland Sound.

At the time of starting out with Jonesee in his canoe, I had no idea where the Kikastan Islands might be or how far. We chugged along under the hundred foot cliffs lining Pangnirtung Fiord for about three hours, myself dressed for warmth in heavy parka and nylon pants that kept falling down. Once or twice we passed rocky islands, with hordes of dogs running along the shore to bark at us frenziedly, wanting to be rescued and perhaps lonesome for human company.

I found out later that Eskimos leave their dogs on islands for the summer, when there's no sled-work to be done. Not all of them, of course. There was a blind husky bitch with white milky eyes and four or five pups with us in the canoe. I inherited the job of hoisting her over the gunwales on landing or embarkation.

A couple of hours after leaving the fiord-mouth and twisting between floating icy rubble in Cumberland Sound, we stopped at another stone island (the same one described in the poem 'Metrics'). But this island was only a hunting camp, and two days later we resumed our journey to the Kikastan Islands. I stayed there for two weeks, camped in a tent with Coleman stove, sleeping bag and groceries.

The settlement in the Kikastans amounted to half a dozen permanent houses, some of them unoccupied and stripped down to bare wooden ribs. There were perhaps a dozen people there, of whom Jonesee and his friend Simonie were the hunters.

I cooked food, slept, wrote, and went with Jonesee on hunting trips a couple of times. And the wind never stopped blowing. Sometimes it shoved icebergs onto the tidal rocks and pounded them to bits. Outside the tent forty or fifty dogs congregated, howling and fighting and crapping. I'd wake from sleep to see their bodies silhouetted against the canvas outside, a few inches away, and think they were trying to get into the tent. In fact, all they did was piss over it. But sometimes, as if at a signal, they'd all howl together, beginning with a small bark or whine, and swelling into such vibrating lunacy you had to clap hands over your ears.

Only once or twice did I feel particularly lonely, and I'm not sure why this should have been so. The feeling has been stronger for me in a city, in Toronto, Montreal and Vancouver, where people feel sheer desperation at times, both economic and personal. But I didn't really have any desperate experiences, and my feeling in all that vastness was oddly regional. Things were new and strange, but not alien. If the Eskimos hadn't been there I couldn't have existed, but within their framework I was comfortable. Only once, when I had a slight fever, did the thought occur that I might have trouble getting back to Pang.

Queerly enough I didn't have the sense of vast and lonely barren distance in the Arctic, even tho it certainly is vast and lonely. Why didn't I? I'm not sure. Perhaps because I looked at things close up, flowers, rivers and people: above all, people. Besides, you'd have a helluva time shoving vast lonely distance into poems.

Anyhow, after two weeks on Jonesee's island I hit the watery road back to Pangnirtung, the Eskimo women standing on the beach to wave goodbye. Jonesee steered his chugging course among the kelp lines and small icebergs, myself freezing to death as usual. I think the weather didn't go below thirty-five or forty degrees while I was there, but it felt like absolute zero to me.

That's about all, I guess. More poems at Pang, a few days waiting for a Canso amphibian that wasn't already overloaded. Half a dozen times I stumbled down to the beach, sweating under a heavy pack, only to find there was no more room on the aircraft.

Mud, mountains and blue water. Unlimited amounts of them. And people of course. Two Norwegian writers whom I met at Frobisher. They were writing a book about the "North West Passage Today" and drank a very good brand of scotch. Jonesee and Simonie, and their families—faces brown as worn pennies, still living up there on the sea islands in Cumberland Sound. And the dogs, migawd yes, the dogs. The hungry howling crapping huskies of Kikastan. I shall think of them occasionally while having long long thoughts in a small cubicle on Roblin Lake.

I could go on and on with this piece, but anything I think important is in the poems. Oh sure, the north is our last frontier etc., which you can read about in other books than mine. Billions in minerals waiting for a guy with geiger counter and geology degree etc. A national purpose for Canada—developing the north, that is. I think this last is probably true, and would mean a great deal to the country—but it remains outside my scope and intent.

About the poems: they seem to me like a set of binoculars thru which you can view the Arctic from several thousand miles away. I'd prefer that the reader felt them to be an extension of his or her own eyes and mind. What I'm doing here is providing my own particular kind of optic glass.

I've worked on the poems for more than a year. Every time they seemed finished and done with, another thought would come. I hope this book is the final exorcism—or do I? There are about fifteen Arctic poems not included here, either because they were bad, or didn't fit into what now seems to me a pattern and integrated whole.

At one time I intended to call the book "Dogsong." But I changed my mind. After the way those dogs treated me I wouldn't give them the satisfaction.

There are many people besides myself responsible for this book. The most important of these has to be The Canada Council, which strangely took a chance that writing poems on an Arctic island wasn't such a crazy idea after all. They supplied the finances. Also Barbara Kilvert and the Hudson's Bay Company, by whose courtesy the paintings of A. Y. Jackson are here reproduced. (Dr. Jackson sees still a different face to the Arctic than myself.) Also the Department of Northern Affairs and National Resources of the Canadian Government. Without their help and co-operation in everything from travel arrangements to housing and Eskimo language interpretation, I might just as well have stayed home in Ameliasburg, Ontario, my original starting point. Also Wayne Morrison, Regional Administrator at Pangnirtung; and Jim Cumming, H.B.C. post manager at Pang. Also Jonesee and his family, on the Kikastan Islands in Cumberland Sound.

A. W. PURDY,
AMELIASBURG, ONT., DECEMBER 1966

Acknowledgements

THE BEAVER
THE CANADIAN BROADCASTING CORPORATION
THE CANADIAN MAGAZINE
DELTA
EVIDENCE
HUDSON'S BAY CO.
NORTH
PARALLEL
PRISM
SATURDAY NIGHT
THE TAMARACK REVIEW
THE VANCOUVER SUN

Unfamiliar Terms and References

THE NORTH WEST PASSAGE *page 20*

'Skraelings' were the natives encountered by Thorfinn Karlsefni on the east coast of North America, as described in the Icelandic sagas. Probably they were Dorset Eskimos.

ARCTIC RIVER *page 22*

The quotation at the beginning of the poem is from C. F. Hall's book, "Life with the Esquimaux", 1865. Hall was an American explorer, discoverer of the Sylvia Grinnell River, which he named after the daughter of his financial sponsor. The Eskimo Thule Culture succeeded the Dorsets, beginning about 900 A.D. to 1750. Thule people were whale-hunters, using the bones for house rafters. They too disappeared, replaced by the modern Eskimo. Both Dorset and Thule people, and their ancestors, figure in Eskimo legends as 'Tunits' or 'Toonjiks', shadowy giants of pre-history. Some 5000 years ago ancestors of the modern Eskimo are thought by archaeologists to have crossed eastward over the Bering Sea on a land or ice bridge, which of course no longer exists.

CANSO *page 34*

The myth of Sedna (and so, alternatively, Nuliayuk and Tallyliyuk) still lives among the Eskimos today, despite the advent of Christianity. In the version I know, Sedna was a beautiful Eskimo girl who lived with her father beside the sea. She enraged him by rejecting all her many suitors. One day when father and daughter were out at sea in their skin boat, a storm came up suddenly. The old hunter thought his daughter was responsible for the storm and threw her overboard, poking out one of her eyes with a paddle and cutting off her fingers when she tried to climb back into the boat.

Sedna's severed fingers miraculously came to life in the water and turned into ocean mammals. She herself sank to the sea-bottom, where she kept many of the animals captive.

Sedna lives there still, on the bottom of the sea, combing her long hair like a princess in a fairy tale, waiting for some previously luckless Eskimo hunter to flatter her into releasing seal and walrus as food for his hungry family. Over the centuries she has somehow managed to acquire a human husband, a soft-hearted hen-pecked man who is continually trying to release the captive animals.

STILL LIFE IN A TENT *page 47*

The passage:
> "pounding motherless bergs
>   to death on rocks
>   stranding the big calves"

                         stems from the fact that glaciers are said to 'calve' when icebergs break off from their sea edges.

ESKIMO HUNTER *page 57*

I'm told that Jonesee, the Eskimo referred to here, was a remarkably efficient hunter, else he would not have possessed all that equipment.

TENT RINGS *page 69*

The term 'angakok' is the Eskimo equivalent of shaman or witch doctor. There are said to be still a few of them in the Arctic, in spite of missionaries.

WHAT DO THE BIRDS THINK? *page 73*

The phrase "bright-over-the-horizon-gazing woman" refers to figureheads on old sailing ships of the last century.